Dear Parents,

Congratulations for choosing a fun and entertaining way to help your child learn to interact with others in pleasing, socially acceptable ways!

Children have the ability to be good, and they are often eager to please. However, they often don't understand their own egocentric or self-centered behavior. This self-centeredness often leads to misbehavior, and the misbehavior often leads to negative responses from others. All too soon, your child can be caught in a destructive cycle of negative action and reaction.

The purpose of the **HELP ME BE GOOD** books is to help your child break the cycle of negative action and reaction. Your child will learn how to replace misbehavior with acceptable behavior. Each **HELP ME BE GOOD** book is designed to do the following in an enjoyable way:

1. Define a misbehavior
2. Explain the cause of the misbehavior
3. Discuss the negative effects of the misbehavior
4. Offer suggestions for replacing the misbehavior with acceptable behavior

While it is effective to read the individual **HELP ME BE GOOD** books when a need arises, the series was designed to follow the normal development of young children. Consequently, presenting the books to your child in the order in which they are listed on the back cover of this book also works well.

As you and your child read the **HELP ME BE GOOD** books, your child will develop good behavior that will help build positive self-esteem and healthy relationships. Reading the books will also help to create a more friendly, happy atmosphere in your home. Thank you for allowing me to be a part of this exciting endeavor!

Sincerely,

Joy Berry

Joy Berry

Published by Joy Berry Enterprises
www.joyberryenterprises.com

A Help Me Be Good Book About

Disobeying

Written By Joy Berry
Illustrated By Bartholomew

This book is about Annie.

Reading about Annie can help you understand and deal with ***disobeying.***

I ASKED YOU NOT TO GET INTO THE COOKIES. I HOPE YOU ARE NOT DISOBEYING ME.
Cookie

You are disobeying when you do not do what you have been told to do.

Your parents have good reasons for telling you what to do. This is why you should not disobey them.

IF YOU EAT A COOKIE NOW, YOU WON'T WANT TO EAT YOUR DINNER.
SIGH!
HOW ABOUT JUST A NIBBLE?

Your parents tell you what to do because they do not want you to hurt yourself or others.

ANNIE! WAIT!
I TOLD YOU NOT TO GO INTO THE STREET!
SCREECH!

Your parents tell you what to do because they do not want you to damage or destroy things.

AUGHHH
I TOLD YOU NOT TO PLAY SO ROUGHLY WITH YOUR THINGS.
I HOPE SHE DOESN'T WANT TO PLAY WITH ME!
GULP!

Your parents tell you what to do because they want you to be liked by other people.

THEY WON'T PLAY WITH ME!
I TOLD YOU THAT YOU HAVE TO BE KIND TO THE OTHER CHILDREN IF YOU WANT THEM TO PLAY WITH YOU.
HMMM... SO THAT'S HOW IT WORKS.

Your parents tell you what to do because they want you to be fair.

I ASKED YOU TO PICK UP YOUR TOYS. IT ISN'T FAIR FOR YOU TO PLAY WITH THE TOYS AND THEN LEAVE THEM FOR SOMEONE ELSE TO PICK UP.
GULP

Sometimes you might wonder why parents get to tell their children what to do.

WHY DO MOM AND DAD GET TO BOSS ME AROUND? WHY CAN'T I BE MY OWN BOSS?
YEAH, **WHY?** JUST BECAUSE THEY'RE BIGGER?
TOYS

Parents tell their children what to do because they have lived longer and have learned more than children.

Thus, parents usually know what is best for their children.

OH NO, ANNIE!
I TOLD YOU NOT TO TOUCH THE HOT STOVE.
EE-OUCH!

Parents tell their children what to do because they are responsible for their children.

Parents have to take care of the damage when their children hurt themselves or others.

HOW MUCH DO I OWE THE DOCTOR FOR TAKING CARE OF ANNIE'S BURN?

Sometimes parents need to punish their children for disobeying.

The purpose of a punishment is to make children feel bad about disobeying so they will not disobey again.

I WISH DAD HADN'T TAKEN MY BIKE AWAY JUST BECAUSE I WAS RIDING IT IN THE STREET! WHEN I GET IT BACK, I WON'T RIDE IT IN THE STREET BECAUSE I DON'T WANT TO HAVE IT TAKEN AWAY AGAIN.

You can avoid being punished if you do these things:

- Talk to your parents.
- Find out what they want you to do. Then do it.

ANNIE, I DON'T WANT YOU TO EAT CANDY BEFORE DINNER.
UH-OH!
DRAT!
CHOCO-BITS

Sometimes you might not agree with your parents. Tell them how you feel.

They might change their minds. If they do not change their minds, drop the subject.

Nagging and throwing tantrums will only frustrate you and make your parents angry.

CAN'T I EAT SOME CANDY BEFORE DINNER, IF I EAT ONLY A LITTLE BIT?
NO! EVEN A LITTLE BIT OF CANDY WILL TAKE AWAY YOUR APPETITE FOR DINNER.
MAYBE I SHOULD HOLD IT UNTIL AFTER DINNER.

Tell the truth if you disobey.

Admit that you disobeyed.

Say that you are sorry and mean it.

DID YOU EAT THIS CANDY?
YES.
YOU SHOULD HAVE LET ME HOLD IT.

Accept your punishment if you disobey.

Do not be angry at your parents when they punish you. Remember, it was you who disobeyed, not them.

Try not to disobey again.

SINCE YOU DISOBEYED, YOU WILL NOT BE ALLOWED TO EAT THE REST OF THE CANDY.
SIGH!
OH, NO.

When you obey, you please your parents, and you are doing what is best for you.

HUG!
GOOD-BYE!

Disobeying Song Lyrics

Music & Lyrics by Joy Berry, Lisa Pétrides & Rita Abrams

Your Parents Are Older and Wiser

Your parents say,
"Be Good, and do what you should."
And there's a reason why.
And there's a reason why.

Your parents are older and wiser,
And they want what's best for you.
So you need to listen to them,
And do what they tell you to do.

When parents punish you,
You don't like them to.
And there's a reason why.
And there's a reason why.

Your parents are older and wiser,
And they want what's best for you.
So you need to listen to them,
And do what they tell you to do.

Your parent's really care,
And want to be fair.
And there's a reason why.
And there's a reason why.

Your parents are older and wiser,
And they want what's best for you.
So you need to listen to them,
And do what they tell you to do.

Your parents say,
"Be good, and do what you should,"
And there's a reason why.
And there's a reason why.

Your parents are older and wiser,
And they want what's best for you.
So you need to listen to them,
And do what they tell you to do.

When parents punish you,
You don't like them to.
And there's a reason why.
And there's a reason why.

Your parents are older and wiser,
And they want what's best for you.
So you need to listen to them,
And do what they tell you to do.

Your parents really care,
And want to be fair,
And there's a reason why.
And there's a reason why.

Your parents are older and wiser,
And they want what's best for you.
So you need to listen to them,
And do what they tell you to do.

When I Disobey

I sit in my room,
crying again.
Feeling as though,
I have lost my best friend.
I've done something wrong.
I disobeyed.
Now I'm feeling alone and afraid.

What should I do?
Oh, what should I say?
I wish I could hide,
Or just run away.

There are times that I feel
That rules don't seem fair.
But I know how much
That my mom and dad care.
When will I see?
The rules are for me,
And it is best when I try to obey.

I knew I was wrong
Before I began.
I wish they could know
Just how sorry I am.
There's no one to blame,
No one but me,
And I'm sorry, as sorry as can be.

What should I do?
Oh what should I say?
It's hard on us all,
When I disobey.

The thing I fear most
Is the hurt in their eyes.
But I know the truth
Is much better than lies.
When will I see?
They're just loving me
When they ask that I try to obey.

Yes, it's best when I try to obey.

Visit us on the web at www.joyberryenterprises.com!

Made in United States
Orlando, FL
12 February 2025

58477528R00021